D0124929

SUSPICIOUS WOUNDS

SUSPICIOUS WOUNDS

POEMS BY

BERNARD HOLLAND

L I A PUBLISHING CO.

NEW YORK, NEW YORK

Acknowledgment is given to Gerri Jackson-Wyatt
for editing this book.

LCCCN: 95-76895

ISBN: 0-9646700-0-3

Manufactured in the United States of America

Published by L I A Publishing Co.
        P.O. Box 5373
        New York, NY 10185-5373

First Printing

To my mother Carolyn,
whose love and friendship
healed my wounds.

How can a man climb
the steps of brotherhood
when he is still crawling
on the floor of jealousy?

The shots of despair
shall ring out
in the theater of life
when apologies prove
to have little meaning.

The sweet taste
of a get-back lick
becomes deadly poisonous
when the consequence
is bitter revenge.

Before we know it
Father Time has taken his scythe
and has slashed our lives
to a mere triviality.

I am sinking

in the quicksand of indecision

struggling to reach

a secure state of mind

on which to advance

toward my chosen destiny.

Doing all

and achieving nothing.

Possessing all

and losing precious dreams.

Living all

and dying tomorrow.

I had my plans mapped out in front of me.

I had my goals written on Life's wall.

Somehow I lost my momentum

while waiting for divine inspiration.

Why can't I mold my dreams?

Why am I still waiting to execute my vision?

I have the knowledge,

I have the desire,

but I am stopped from becoming great

by running out of something

I never thought to save.

A steel blade

has not lacerated this mortal frame

nor has one drop of blood departed

from these life flowing veins

but the pain I endure

has killed all my emotions

for I have been Judas kissed.

Not by Man but by his Lord;

that ever fleeting always

leaving obscurity called Time.

I told my life story

but no one remembers it.

I expressed my deepest feelings

but no one heard a single emotion.

I sang the essence of my being

but no one understood its rhythm.

I shouted the passion in my soul

but no one was moved to embrace me.

Is speech necessary?

No one listens.

Once a person speaks

their words fly to the stratosphere

circling the globe for eons.

Why keep a diary?

Listen to the wind

and you'll hear your own thoughts!

I am grateful that you call everyday.

No one else is concerned about me.

I need to hear your nosy questions.

I feel at ease knowing that you care.

People believe that I don't need any help

but you keep asking if everything is okay.

You should worry about me;

I am in great spirits.

I am at the peak of my mental acumen,

my adrenaline is flowing

and I am ready to tackle anything

that comes my way.

Yes, please worry about me

because I fantasize

that I've got it all under control.

I don't need a lover,
I need a friend.
I don't need pleasure,
I need to feel accepted.
I don't need a commitment,
I need to be acknowledged.
I don't need satisfaction,
I need to be heard.

When I speak my mind
everyone backs off
with a closed mind and says:
"It's beyond me!"
without opening their eardrums.

All I want
is a sympathetic ear,
a sense of interest,
a slap in the face.
Anything besides silence!

The world will not get the best of me
for I know a place
where humanity cannot find me.
I can block out negativity
and turn away pessimism
at the door of my mind.
Evil won't be able to find me
because it can't survive where I hide.
The multitude can press against my soul
but never damage the divinity within me.
I have found peace within a shell,
it is my tear filled sanctuary.
I listen to my wondrous thoughts
contented with my loneliness.
I've no desire for friendships,
no shoulders are strong enough to lean on.
Encouraging words are extinct;
fortitude must come from within.

Talking in the midst of void.

Listening to empty words murdering thought.

Learning false wisdom on society's sinking ship.

Exchanging ideas at the bottom of a dead river.

I feel isolated.

Removed from the human race

with no other mind to communicate with.

A planet without a sun.

A God without believers.

A life without life.

My presence on Earth is no longer necessary.

I have failed to achieve communion.

Pitty-pitty pat-pat,

pitty-pitty pat-pat,

die villain die!

Thump-beat, thump-beat,

thump-beat-thump,

tear the chest open,

rip it wide apart!

Hang-ho, hang-ho,

put it in a bucket,

put it in a bucket,

all the blood and guts!

Walk the earth?

No!

Be alive?

No!

Exist?

No!

Not for me,

not for me,

I haven't any right!

My balloons!

Where are my balloons?

My little pink balloons.

I must hold them in my hands

so I can fly off to a distant world

that lies between the clouds.

I must make my journey now

for someone is out to do me in.

My balloons!

Where are my balloons?

My little pink balloons.

You can't change circumstances.

Don't knock yourself crazy

thinking about what might have happened

had you done this instead of that.

You must bear the consequences of your actions.

You must maintain a positive frame of mind

after those circumstances explode in your face

leaving you emotionally wounded and scarred.

I don't know what's wrong with me.

I have to stop breaking down.

I must be in control of my emotions.

I try

but I've never felt this way before.

My entire body feels helpless

and my mind unhinged

as though I am lost in a maze

which is being filled with sand

by some unknown force.

It frightens me.

I am struggling

yet I don't know with what.

If I only knew my mysterious opponent

I could fight back.

Meet it eye to eye

and overcome this weight

that is dragging me down

to a state of mental feebleness.

I am sorry,

I just don't understand.

I hear your thoughts

but they have no meaning for me.

They're far apart from who I am

and from who I thought you were.

You have become a stranger to me

in body, mind and spirit

whom I can't help or console.

Maybe if your thoughts weren't so selfish

you wouldn't be up all night

looking for a friend

to help you fight your delusions.

Everyone tries to understand me

like it was some amusement park game

where for a quarter you get three tries.

I don't want anyone to understand.

It's impossible for others to comprehend

my unique feelings and emotions;

my signet of individuality that sets me apart

from the multitude of Homo-Sapiens.

No one must ever understand me.

I must always keep everyone guessing.

If I am ever understood,

I am done for!

Why am I showing my hostility?

Must I express violence?

Can't my intellect override my rage?

Will animosity become my dominant emotion?

Will my goodness fade into bitterness?

Despair shines once more.

The night which was quiet and peaceful

is slowly breaking up

to make way for the violent and deadly rays

of the morning sun.

Death is to come!

Yesterday I cried upon my pillow.

This morning I was weeping in my hands.

By tonight tears will stain my cheeks.

I'll never know the true meaning of sorrow.

I cry for no one else but me.

I fell as I was walking toward my destiny.

I slipped on my own sense of importance.

The weight of my ego is keeping me down.

I can't remember how to be humble.

Is it too late to get up on my feet and love?

A December snowflake

falls from the heavens

on a humid August morning

attempting to cool the fiery hatred

that burns within the souls

of hostile Adamites.

Life is just one moment after another;

no planned destiny or meaningful correlation.

The Will of God is a sham!

There are moments of despair and moments of joy

linked together to create a haphazard existence.

Let's be grateful that for most of our lives

we've been fortunate enough to experience the joy.

Let's be content with that.

They tell me to stop dreaming.

They tell me to quit kidding myself.

They tell me to accept reality.

They tell me to grow up

but I won't listen to them.

I will not be afraid to explore

new areas that are within my grasp.

I am not going to spend my entire life

sailing a smooth and safe course

until I reach death.

I am going to ride the tidal waves,

buffet the storms

and follow the hurricane winds

until I fall off the end of the world.

You disappointed her,

I disappointed her,

the whole world has disappointed her.

No one she knew had the guts

to help make her vision come true.

She died because no one believed in her,

no one would give their all for her.

She was a better person than we will ever be.

She's gone to a place

where the faithful live the reality

proportionate to their dreams.

You didn't love me.

You loved being flattered.

You loved the attention I gave you.

You loved being my idol.

If you had really loved me

you would have been able to save me

for true love has the power to heal.

Why do you look at me with somber eyes
as if your heart wishes to die of despair?
Are you afraid to express the grief you feel
or does your intellectual nature
tell you that a mask should be worn
to hide humanity's universal tribulation?
A mask may hide the mouth, nose and forehead
but the eyes peer out to the world
crying out the human tragedy of loneliness.

I want your companionship.

I want you to tell me all your problems

and your secret thoughts.

I want to listen and try to help.

Your problems are my problems,

your frustrations are my frustrations,

your disappointments are my disappointments.

Talk to me.

Don't ever be afraid to talk to me.

Don't ever go to anyone else.

Come to me

and let me comfort you.

Let me ease your pain.

The concern and understanding
that you give to another person
comes back to you
in that person reaching out
for your help and support.
What greater feeling can there be
than that of being needed?

We can never again live by any sort of morals.

Why bother?

They're obsolete!

What's the good in having a sense of morality

if it is abandoned when we need it the most?

We passed the buck.

We are to blame.

We caused the loss of life.

We were negligent in our obligation

to keep the angel of death from striking.

We will always possess hypocrisy.

Morality doesn't stand a chance to survive.

The Lord wrote the Holy Word upon the ground

for the benefit of those who were illiterate.

Therefore the bishops could not read it

for they were ignorant in the language of God.

There's no justification to our lives.

There's no longer any compassion in our hearts.

Cold steel is warmer than our kindness.

Our souls are numbed by resentment.

We are zombies who walk the earth

trying to find the way back to love.

Why is it so important

that we do anything worthy?

We can't save the world.

We can't abolish evil.

We can't change society for the better.

We can't even do the grocery shopping.

We are just a bunch of lazy people

basking in the peace that is shining on us.

We know how to enjoy life.

We don't worry about anything!

You can always leave
this luxurious den of waste
that I have painstakingly
provided for you.
Go!
Pack your bags and go.
I don't want my decadent lifestyle
to corrupt your sense of worthiness.
But before you go just remember this.
You can't possibly change
the extravagant way
that you are used to living.
It's in your blood
and you can't cough it up.
You'll be back when you realize
that there is no virtue
in being respectable.

You spoiled her.

You catered to her every whim

and pampered her with luxury.

You made life too soft and easy for her.

What did you expect?

She can't face her problems now

because you never gave her a chance

to ever have a problem.

You tried to give her happiness

and she ended up in despair.

Put your money away.

You can't buy her what she needs.

Hope is a commodity

which is only given

by the grace and glory of Heaven.

Why are friends alien to me?

Why can't I speak the language of comradeship?

Must I be enchanting and entertaining?

Is wit the requirement to be invited out?

Is small talk the universal key to popularity?

Must I quote exaggerated anecdotes to be sociable?

Why can't people communicate more honestly?

Has sincerity in conversation become a lost art?

How much longer must I listen to people

talk about their delusions of an exciting life?

When will I meet a person who has the guts to say:

"I like you because you're as boring as me."?

Love struck me out

on a slow passionate curve.

I stand at the plate

with the game of infatuation lost.

I missed my chance and my opportunity.

I lost my quest for happiness.

Why didn't I swing

when ardor passed my erogenous zone?

Why did I hopelessly wait

for love to throw devotion straight?

I am a dream

abandoned in the Siberia of human will.

Lost forever

between hope's desire and greed's passion.

I was born

by the exuberance and excitement of youth.

Now I am dying

by the cynical thoughts of middle age ambition.

There was a day

when I ruled a man's thoughts and destiny.

Sensibility's knights

have robbed me of my throne and kingdom.

As the hours pass we think of poetics.

Lost in a world of images,

we accept frustration as part of our art.

Being fools who hoped the world

could be conquered with a song,

we discovered there was no place

to recite our lyrics.

Our fate is to always be stifled

until the trumpet blows

which will signal the end of our creativity.

Why did we believe

that our poems would be appreciated?

Those who will treasure our language

are not yet born.

You don't walk away from a relationship
just because there are times of aloofness.
Sometimes love has to be recharged;
not with sheer emotion
but with rational thinking.
Say what you have to say.
Get the frustrations out.
Know the truth about each other
believing that hostile feelings
will become mellow
and love will prevail in the end.
Time is the greatest healer
but you must be patient.
You must cry a thousand hours
before a single tear reaches the heart
of the one that you love.

On the day I entered kindergarten

my peaceful life was changed for the worse.

The contentment of my preschool years

became a fading memory of the good old days.

The protective shell in which I lived

was bombarded

by the troublesome missiles of society.

No longer was I to be alone;

friends and companionship were to be attained.

The art of conversation was to be learned

and the idea of sharing

was the principle to be taught.

Fun and games with other children awaited me

inside P.S. 182 five blocks away

but in reality sociability for me

was a million miles away;

a lifetime away;

an eternity away.

Morning-morning, beautiful morning.

The hope for love dwells

in a lonely teenager's heart.

Morning-morning, wonderful morning.

Should Aphrodite's passion

possess one so young?

Morning-morning, graceful morning.

Infatuation for a lover

has overwhelmed all thoughts of Mother.

Morning-morning, joyful morning.

Expectations to receive affection

make the youth laugh with hysteria.

Morning-morning, cheerful morning.

The desire to make romantic dreams come true

gives an unfledged life

a purpose it never had before.

At eighteen I possessed optimistic eyes

which dreamed visions of romantic bliss

and sought compassion in a pessimistic world.

At twenty-one I possessed cynical eyes

which cried themselves to sleep in a lonely bed

and became blind to the love within their sight.

I'll get there when I get there.

There's no need to hurry.

I won't miss anything exciting.

Where I am going won't disappear.

I'll get there when I get there.

My second act has just begun.

I won't mind being late.

My show will end once I arrive.

I'll get there when I get there.

I want to enjoy each cherished moment.

I want to live the fullest life.

I want to see today if not tomorrow.

I'll get there when I get there.

I hear my song in the distance.

The melody I heard when I was born.

I wish to write the lyrics before I die.

I am going to give the world my love today.

I am going to love all the selfish people.

I am going to love all the arrogant people.

I am going to love all the spiteful people.

I am going to love all the hateful people.

I am going to love all the angry people.

I am going to love all the cruel people.

I am going to love all the vain people.

I am going to love all the malicious people.

I am going to love all the cold-hearted people.

I am going to love all the unlovable people.

I am going to receive the love of the world
by loving first.

We spend our entire existence

ignoring the life time consumes from us.

Minute by minute whisk by

without us having any sense of accomplishment.

We are born, live off the fat and then die.

Nothing worthwhile is ever done.

We tell ourselves there will be more time tomorrow

to accomplish those tasks that are truly important

but when tomorrow comes we're so caught up

in trying to live the "Good Life,"

we don't realize that the day we've been waiting for

to turn over a new leaf is here and passing.

We live for tomorrow

with no true comprehension of today.

Off we go prancing around carefree,

thinking all the while that time is standing still.

We keep kidding ourselves by convincing ourselves

we'll get serious and be productive by tomorrow.

I never said I was religious

but I pray when I am weak.

I pray when I fall to my vices.

I pray when I need strength.

I pray when I feel that I can't go on

because I am too tired from all the hurt.

I pray to keep from crying.

I pray for light to enter my darkened soul.

I pray for the patience to lead a decent life

while bearing my disappointments with grace.

I pray for enough love to love myself.

Have you spoken to the blind man?

Did you tell him all your troubles?

I bet he listened without interrupting

and gave a silent nod of sympathy.

It's quite amazing how he follows what you say

considering he's totally deaf.

I guess some people can feel our vibes

with a tender and loving caress of the hand.

The way he gives encouragement and hope

while uttering beastly sounds,

is more poetic than the Bible

for it comes from the heart and soul.

This man is a human treasure,

he should have been a presidential advisor.

I am sorry to say he died last night;

a bum, a drunkard, a saint.

I resent other people

reaping the fruits of my tribulation.

I was the one who was always there

to listen to your goals and aspirations.

I gave you the strength you needed

to stick with it.

I had faith in you.

I believed in your abilities,

not your friends.

All they ever gave you

was a pat on the back.

I supported your back and held you up

when you cried like a baby,

whining that you couldn't go on

and that you were going to quit.

I made you believe in yourself.

I kept your hopes alive.

If it wasn't for my determination

to see you succeed,

you wouldn't be a superstar!

I'll say bye to this lonely life;
it has no merit or just cause.
Sorrow is its painful outcome;
happiness is drowned by gray tears.
Solitude creates empty dreams,
barren hopes, wasted lives.
The only gain is self-pity
which sinks us faster than quicksand.
I'll change my ways and views on life
for I now have love to live by.
I have a lover who is my friend
therefore being alone is past.

What tunnel is this I am in

that prevents me from having friends?

There is no light nor is there sound,

just a deadly feeling of void.

I can walk on forever more

and never reach a human soul.

I am by myself as usual,

living a lonely existence.

I am puzzled at this moment,

I do not truly understand.

Why do I have an empty life

when people are all around me?

Can't I sleep and dream forever?

Must I awake to face the day?

There is nothing but frustration;

all my hopes are suffocating.

Depression fills my existence;

suicide is thought of daily.

Why go through the motions of life

when nothing ever turns out right?

In my dreams all things go my way;

I am happy, gay and carefree.

I hope I never do wake up;

reality is a nightmare.

I told Mother I was tired;

frustration has made life weary.

Disillusion clutters the mind;

each day is darker than a grave.

Boredom has replaced lofty dreams;

inspiring hopes have vanished.

The glory of Man is a farce;

people are as ordinary as dirt.

Mother stopped me from complaining;

she spoke a truth that woke me up.

"The whole goddamn world is tired;

 that's how you can tell you're alive!"

An autumn moonbeam pierced my heart

freezing my hatred to blue frost.

Gone is my ability to love,

Cupid's arrow cannot melt ice.

Warmth is now alien to me,

my days are dark, cold and lonely.

The storm inside me is wintry,

withering away my kindness.

I am restricted to one emotion

because I practiced it the most.

The hate I bear is killing me,

my life has been chilled to a void.

I am stuck in a crack on the street;

can't move my feet a simple stride;

not an inch to the left or right;

doomed to live my life on West Fourth.

Since I am here I might as well write;

my thoughts may be of some interest.

Bring me a pen

and lots of paper if you please.

Can't squander any precious time;

don't know how long I'll be around.

I may get stepped on pretty soon

then be swept away by death's broom.

His marriage was to libation

and his wife was the bottle quart.

His son was a pint of bourbon

and his daughter was demon rum.

He ignored the life he sired

for a drop of white lightning's flash.

His family would have been sold

for the price of a cup that cheers.

He was a wino who became a lush;

a broken and burned-out boozer.

He was no minister of mine;

just a damned dried up whisky stain.

Think the ultimate fantasy;

live in a world of make-believe.

See the impossible at work;

turn sensible logic bizarre.

Use your wild imagination;

surpass Alice's wonderland.

Hypnotize yourself with daydreams;

create your own weird universe.

Forget all problems and troubles;

take a vacation from your woes.

Don't delay this magical trip;

just pack up your fancies and go.

When I was five I was content;

religion was not in my life.

At six I had to attend church;

the whole thing was a holy drag.

By eight I fell in love with God;

the feeling was sincere and pure.

Religious teaching came at nine;

everything I did was a sin.

Stress developed at eleven;

the Church stifled my love for God.

When I was twelve I wasn't content;

religion was in my life.

Let me float in a stream all year

two feet wide and six inches deep.

Lying on my back without cares

dissolving into cool waters.

Letting sunlight stroke my wet skin

like a long lost lover in bed.

Feeling a breeze tickling my nose

which makes me smile with contentment.

Watching birds dance above my head

while listening to guppies sing.

If the stream should ever dry up

I'll cry until I float once more.

Were you ever bullied around
or laughed at every single day?
Did your classmates play tricks on you
or exclude you from all their games?
Were you too shy to be with people
or too afraid to say hello?
Did the pimples conquer your face
or terrify all friends away?
Were you a frustrated virgin
or a masturbational nerd?
Did the thought of suicide come
or was the will to live too strong?

The bluebird chirped a melody
written by a silver-winged dove.
The graceful notes filled the air
hypnotizing sparrows in flight.
Orioles and skylarks turned white,
the sound purified their bodies.
Majestic eagles cried "Bravo"
then fainted from the splendidness.
Robins danced atop silken clouds
in a celebration of joy.
The stratosphere became Heaven
on the day God created Man.

I danced a waltz with her but once;

my head was filled with ecstasy.

I held her by the waist but once;

an orgasm was promptly felt.

I kissed her tender lips but once;

the mark of Cupid was branded.

I hugged her with passion but once;

my body melted into hers.

I gazed into her eyes but once;

the result was infatuation.

I spoke my love to her but once;

my heart cried for she loved me not.

If there are many galaxies

why can't there be many Gods?

Each with an unique behavior

or strange personality quirk.

Maybe our God is senile

or just simply absent-minded.

For it seems He can't find us,

lost His map of the Milky Way.

He's possibly searching for Earth

but can't recall just where we are.

Don't blame Him for getting lost,

let's remember He's only God.

The unlit candle shined the truth

creating a hellish darkness.

The wax was easily melted

by the fierce heat of Man's anger.

Satan would have felt quite at home

during this meeting of nations.

Hate electrified the air;

ill-will traveled faster than light.

A treaty was the hopeful goal;

war was the desired wish.

The men talked, listened, nodded,

then shook hands

but the dove was left in her cage.

People do not really want peace;

it's a word that is only said.

The coming together of the planet

pleases not a single person.

The idea of a passive world

is not taken seriously.

Where would society be

if hate did not show its color?

There would be no wars or conflicts;

life would be simple and pleasant.

War shall live on and on.

Who wants to live in dull peace?

Oh brotherhood, Oh brotherhood.

Where art thou hiding in this world?

I cannot see you or touch you;

my life seems lost in a sandstorm.

Shouldn't you be glowing brightly,

shedding your light upon each soul?

Where do I turn to learn your faith?

How can I believe in Mankind?

Are trust and love flimsy words

or are they etched in stone somewhere?

Say you lie within my heart

and I'll be your pulpit for life.

Whispering waves tell their sad tales;

seagulls hum an old love ballad.

The fog weeps for a dream that died;

a crab recites Man's requiem.

Turtles discuss Shakespeare's writing;

violins are played by dolphins.

Sand pebbles scream a woeful cry;

God's words are preached by clouds above.

These sounds are heard only at dawn

on a beach when alone in prayer.

It is the soul that hears all;

the intellect of Man is deaf to life.

The sky has fallen down on the masses;

dropped like an avalanche of snow.

The clouds are now touching the ground;

blue heavens are lofty no more.

The weight has crushed each inch of land;

nothing to speak of is standing.

All people are buried alive;

the firmament a common grave.

Each soul has died without a prayer;

they did not listen to Chicken Little.

The cry was called but no one cared;

love was thought to be immortal.

An imaginary sunset fades;

doomsday has reached its twelfth hour.

Dark becomes death dressed in yellow;

the sands of time turn into blood.

Pain bites laughter square on the throat;

despair quickly becomes the vogue.

Tomorrow has canceled its show;

skeletons applaud from their graves.

Judgment was passed without mercy;

Gabriel whistles a solemn tune.

People commit suicide in droves;

young poets write down their last thoughts.

The moon cries out for a friend.

He was born a lovesick loner

wandering aimlessly through Cupid's universe

searching for a companion who cares.

Can't you hear him sighing in despair?

Don't you see his melancholy countenance?

He's been alone for a thousand years

with only his ardent desires for company.

Please wave hello to the moon;

look into his eyes and see his dreams.

Please blow a kiss to the moon;

listen to the music of a solitary romantic.

The moon is an outcast, a gypsy, a poet

who sings his lyrics while the world beats him.

Yet he'll provide grace, elegance and beauty

for anyone kind enough to sit on his crescent

and laugh away his agonizing sorrow.

The moon is a paradise in the cosmos

where love will never die or be forgotten.

The moon is not a desolate sphere of rock.

He's a compassionate man no one understands,

waiting for a maiden who will fondle his heart.

The heart of honesty was knifed,

stabbed with the dagger of deceit.

Truth is now dying of its wounds,

the blood of faith has formed a pool.

Honor was cut down in its prime,

brutally murdered just for spite.

Probity is crying in despair,

she has no one to defend her.

Mankind has lost his sacred jewel,

tomorrow's ethics will be false.

What will now become of virtue,

integrity and righteousness?

Picture Man without his conscience,

God may wash His hands of us all.

Who is to blame for this foul deed?

Come, come, be honest and speak up.

Cracking the sky into thirds forgetting the whole,

thunder hugs an olive branch atop Mount Fuji.

Lovers recite words which vanish in the wind

trying to remember a moonbeam now lost.

Wishing on a rainbow colored star

about to explode,

marble hearts crumble

because they have sinned.

As raindrops erase tears

carved into the bark of trees,

old lovers glide on brass beds

slipping through keyholes.

Who dares kidnap a princess

for daffodils and daisies

while flying seahorses

whip mashed potatoes on ice?

Pulling rosary out of virgin eggshells wet,

mother shark suffocates while mating in the tide.

A child's valentine lies in the gutter abandoned,

tossed away for the world to see and cry.

The world must have a new beginning,

a new time, a new place.

The past cries out to be relived

while the future waits to destroy Mankind.

Mother Earth has lost control of her children

for she pleads to be respected,

she begs to be loved,

she dies when no one answers.

The stars in the universe have suddenly vanished

while the moon sings a sad song

to end its nightly engagement.

The time is now in place.

The place is now out of time.

No one sees, no one hears

but the deaf and blind shall reign!

A tornado not made of wind but love
has destroyed a foundation of marriage.
The house still stands but ready to collapse
for the wife has found a new attraction.
Conjugal obligations mean nothing;
wedding vows are just faintly heard echoes.
She desires to be near her honey
but her hubby is not the bee who stings her.
The yearning she has for her new found love
passes the realm of eroticism.
She is afraid yet she is excited;
her sexual awareness has blossomed.
Home cannot satisfy her urgent needs;
a new bed must be conquered and enjoyed.
Serenading songs were the enticement;
she will move an inch in her stymied life.
Guilt has been melted away to a speck;
a decision has been engraved in stone.
The bond with her spouse must be broken;
her independence is her cherished dream.
But has she the nerve, has she the courage
to proclaim she's in love with a fantasy?

Life!

I have been revitalized

by the potency of dazzling life.

I am high on the feeling of

exuberance and vivacity.

I am bubbling over from the heat of pizazz.

I've got enough oomph

to last me until my dying day.

Don't need no heroin and don't need no coke

for I've already overdosed

on the pills of zeal and zest.

The fervor rises to make my head giddy

and I scream from the pain of pleasurable joy.

The appetite for gaiety is insatiable

so I am hooked on this drug called fun.

Don't try to save me by curing this addiction;

just let me dance to the music

of Life's ragtime song.

Wrapped around snugly her angelic arms,
heartbeats crash entangling passion.
One moment dreamt nightly for years,
nipples tear flesh with love's blazing sword.
Lady chest wrecks havoc,
Sir chest succumbs,
masculinity becomes feminine
overshadowing Amazonians.
Milk flows through souls nourished by a kiss,
strangers become companions
sewn together at the heart.
Breath suspends,
a whisper circulates air made of light.
Exotic scent tingles the skin made laughing;
lust replaces love in the back alley of desire.
Bodies eaten slowly,
eternal libidos devoured forever.
Happiness found,
caressing new friend aglow.
Gentle thanks,
unspoken thoughts embraced.

Hello Momma.

Your child has become a hard and bitter person.

My wounds are healed

but the ugly emotional scars of life

have deformed my beautiful soul for eternity.

Can I come back home?

You were right Momma,

the big city was no place for someone

of my religious background and upbringing.

I should have listened to you

and stayed in your decent town after graduation

instead of seeking sophistication and glamour

with people who were no good for me.

I've learned my lesson Momma.

Can you forgive your child for leaving you?

Can I come back home?

I now have the patience

to lead a simple country life.

I am not restless any longer.

My experiences have taught me how to find peace

in the things I used to find so boring.

I can now be contented and happy.

I am more like you than you think.

We can be such good friends.

There's still time for us to be close.

Can I come back home?

There's no longer any reason

for you to be ashamed of me.

What separated us years ago is no longer a reality.

Can't we pretend it never happened?

Can't we think of it as a bad dream?

Can't we begin a past life

without remembering the past?

Momma, can I please come back home?

Nina, sweet and loving Nina.

I quiver at the thought of her name

for it intoxicates the cerebrum of passion.

She represents the finest treasure

people can hold dear to their hearts.

Gold becomes hollow and rubies rust

when compared to Nina's worth.

Her riches give me vivid images to stir the soul.

I am not ashamed to trumpet my love for her.

She is a dove, a lamb,

a budding debutante in the spring of my mind.

Thoughts of her

create a seizure of euphoria within my body

which removes all desire of life's necessities.

Let me stand naked in the world

for my worship of Nina

shall clothe me in love laced with infatuation.

She is a mark of supreme beauty

grown on a puss infected world.

People look to her for relief

from the eyesores of a decaying society.

All foregoing beauty
was a prelude to her loveliness;
grace has now a new standard.
Any fairy would hide her face in shame
if stood on Nina's shoulder.
Mermaids and nymphs are thought of as old hags
once eyes are set on Nina.
There is no rival to challenge her
in Aphrodite's game.
The air around her is pure,
the ground she walks on turns holy.
Her personality establishes a new religion
and I am blessed because of my love for her.
I would cry blood and sell my soul
that I may be close to Nina.
A touch by her hand is gentler
than a cool mist tickling the cheeks
and her breath sprays sweet poison to the mind
for it overwhelms all sense of logic.
Madly in love is a cliché
I'll repeat ten times ten lifetimes.

Her lustrous silken complexion

gleams in the radiance of the sun

which gives the impression of a goddess

walking in the realm of Heaven.

Her angelical voice

sings out a melody of harmony

which may put eagles to sleep in mid-flight.

She has a humble smile

that will bring new life to any condemned being

and her pupils are black holes of the universe,

ensnaring all towards her to a blissful existence.

She is a kind and winsome creature

whose goodness bestrides her virtue.

I live for Nina to dwell in her innocence!

Dancing on a daisy suspended in Niagara,
a Jamaican smile replaces the Sun
above the North Pole.
Holding Jupiter in my hand I leap beyond Pluto
while three dimensional rainbows
disappear within my ear.
I blush, turning the sky a cardinal quilt
embarrassed for rehashing Pygmalion's emotions.
My heart plays jazz backed by a Beethoven beat
bursting Cupid's cocoon
created by elves in the night.
Aphrodite's spell turns my blood lascivious lava
erupting sapphire sap
from the bowels of erotic trees.
Imaginary eyes handcuff lips with a mute song
serenading sensual tornadoes
gyrating on a butterfly's wing.
Supernovas shade their faces
from the brilliance of my aura
while passionate desires
parachute within fantasy's fire.

Bodies!

Those dainty, delicate, distaff physiques.

They drift, they sail,

they float about in a dream-like state.

No frail pirouettes or flawed cabrioles

for they are supreme ballerinas.

All elements working together

to attain a Rembrantesque reaction.

Heads held higher than majestic peacocks

daring the world to find one fault.

Torsos fragile and feeble to the untrained eye

transgressing the finesse of Herculean athletes.

Legs prancing around in all directions

able to fly through the heavens

without disturbing cosmic dust.

Feet gliding on air

to reach perfection of a graceful swan.

Arms moving to and fro

wavering in the essence of a perfumed stage.

Pelvises twisting and turning

in gyroscope resemblance

surrounding infinite space with flesh filled glory.

The dance creates an artistic orgasm

able to transcend minds

to the mystical regions of enchantment.

Reality has no meaning,

life possesses no logic,

for the psyche is in another world;

floating on a star in a river called Imagintasia.

I could always sense

my spiritual unity with the track.

The track was closer to me than my soul

and I knew it as a dear friend

with an amiable personality.

The track was a personification of myself,

dedicated to the pursuit of athletic excellence.

On the track I streaked faster

than a graceful cheetah in the wilds of Africa.

The track was my second home.

I visited the track daily, rain or shine,

soaking up the vibrations of the Earth's energy

which permeated the oval.

I would caress the track with my bare feet

and admire it with infatuation.

The track was definitely a "she"

who seduced me with a coquettishly enticing aroma

that intoxicated me into spending hours on end

in the presence of her company.

To me the track was a living entity.

It breathed, it had a heartbeat, it laughed,

it showed compassion, it cried in sympathy

and understood the pursuit of a dream.

It had a memory that a runner could tap into.

I could recall all the strides I ever muscled out;

hear every drop of sweat

that fell from my forehead

staining the ground like blood on a battlefield;

smell the ecstasy of my victories

rising from the surface

and taste the passion of harmony

as I ran in tempo with the pulse of the track.

Running was my religion

and the track was where I worshipped.

Have you ever wanted to be a child again?

When life was simple and uncomplicated?

When the imagination was at its creative zenith?

When make-believe took the place of harsh reality?

Many times I've wished for the opportunity

to relive the happiest years of my life.

Everything was exciting then.

The things I now take for granted

were all new adventures to be explored

during those days

when God took a back seat to Santa Claus.

Every hour seemed to last forever

and death had no meaning for life had just begun.

To be an adult was just a fantasy

and the entire world revolved around me.

Pain was only a bruise on the knee

and the feeling of despair

was dropping an ice cream cone.

Life was full of pleasures then

and all troubles were forgotten

after a movie and a game of tag.

There was love and there was affection.

Being content was as natural as breathing air

and all needs were satisfied without even asking.

Come to think of it,

smiling the next day was more guaranteed

than the rising of the sun.

Laughter was the cry of the time

and play was the philosophy of life.

Why can't a child remain a child

and live in a world of innocence forever?

Why must the imagination fade

to be taken over by logic and reason?

Why must happiness now be just a wish

and not felt as it once was?

Why is Nature so cruel

to quickly take away those hours

that used to last forever?

Why did I ever have to grow up?

No matter how frustrating life becomes,

peace is to be found in the sky.

This thought comforted Father

when he looked out the window of his study.

There was never anything spectacular about the sky.

There were never any rainbows

or amusing cloud formations.

The sky was plain and ordinary.

No one else in my family

ever bothered to glance up at it

yet Father contemplated the sky often.

The sky provided him with strength

because it forever endures.

No matter what problem confronted Father

the sky was there to say:

"Hey pal, take it easy.

Don't fret, relax.

Take everything in stride.

Nothing is worth crying over.

It's not the end of the world

because I am still here.

I've been around for a few billion years

and I am planning to stick around

for a few billion more.

I've been polluted and raped by Man

but I am still here.

I too am tired, frustrated and depressed

but I won't roll over and die

because Mother Nature blessed me by creating me.

I may be scarred but I am grand and majestic.

I protect the Earth from the deadly rays of the Sun

and I provide rain that sustains life.

I am the mighty heavens.

I am supreme.

I shall endure.

When the day comes when I exist no more,

I shall have no regrets

for I have achieved greatness by simply being."

This is why Father felt peace

when he looked up at the sky.

He was a human being.

He too was great for existing.

He would endure!

All trials and tribulations were finished.

It was a peaceful time to relish and savor.

There was nothing more to study.

All the world's knowledge was known

and the thought of learning anything new

was beyond their comprehension.

It was a time to relax

and enjoy the deserved respect.

The entire senior class was on a perpetual siesta,

strutting their laurels

by laughing and singing in the courtyard.

Anxiety was now taken over by nostalgia

as they reminisced their school experiences

with the flair of old time war veterans.

The final semester was better than

playing tag on roller skates with best friends.

There was fun, jocularity and mirth.

There was a feeling that the soul

had been released from Hell

and now flew higher than the golden phoenix

into the glory of Heaven.

There was a new found freedom

of the will and mind.

There was joy and a happiness for living.

It was time to be a kid for the last time

before the trials and tribulations

of adulthood began.

There was no thought of tomorrow.

There was only the Eternal Now

of being a youth forever.

There was a sense of totality and fulfillment.

They had passed the test of a modern day initiation.

Four years ago they were naive freshmen.

Now they were sophisticated and worldly graduates

with the taste of success in their hearts

ready to tackle civilization

and do better than their parents.

They could never be frustrated

or know the meaning of failure.

The world laid at their feet to conquer.

Why should they be concerned about the future?

Success was theirs!

"Where did you learn how to kiss?" she asked.

"It's unusual for a young man

to possess so much flair.

You kiss with the expertise of a womanizer,

the passion of a Romeo and the lust of a gigolo

yet you say you've never had a girl or been in love.

You call yourself a loner

who leads a monastic life."

"Where did you learn how to kiss?" she asked.

"How do you know the exact spot

to place your tongue?

Your kisses send chills up my spine

and leave me breathless.

Who gave you the insight

to play with a woman's lips?

You lick without shame and suck with perversion.

Why were you so shy and forced me to kiss first?"

"Where did you learn how to kiss?" she asked.

"Your kisses are addicting,

I lie awake at night anticipating the next smack.

Surely you've done this a thousand times

with a thousand different women,

yet there's a newness in every one of your kisses.

Where have you been?

Whom have you been with?

I thought you were a virgin whom I could excite."

"Where did you learn how to kiss?" she asked.

"How can you be tender and wicked

at the same time?

I am a mature woman

with years of romance behind me,

yet I feel like a teenage girl

who's been kissed for the first time.

I experience the haunting cry within you

to express your love.

The sensation of your loneliness

exhilarates me to a climax."

"Where did you learn how to kiss?" she asked.

"I refuse to believe that you learned from a dream!"

Why must the innocent be crushed

by the stony vices of Man?

They do no harm, they do no wrong

yet they are forever being drawn

into distressful and bewildering states of affairs

brought on by Satan's desecrated deeds.

They cannot escape

from these devilish whirlpools of human destruction

for their strength is evaporated

and their courage is dissolved

by the pain which overwhelms and paralyzes

the flimsy and transparent psyche.

Why do the innocent bleed?

Why are they hurt by the shortcomings of others?

What is the purpose in the suffering of fluff?

Is there need, is there cause, is there help?

Is there pity by those who watch in vain?

Let the world take note;

Nature holds no patience

for this onslaught on chaste souls.

It is not pious; it is not sanctifiable.

The sparrow chirps static to show its contempt

and the butterfly cries a teardrop

drowning in its sorrow.

The skies become darker

to eclipse the darkness of evil

and the mountains grow higher

to prove the insignificance of Man

beyond his breed.

Who knows the answer to this enigmatic question?

Why is it that one thousand virtuous men

can only achieve one inch of righteousness,

while only one immoral man

can achieve one thousand miles of malefaction?

This injustice must eventually be dealt with.

The only way to solve the problems of life

is to fight the problems of life.

One day Nature will strike away the cancer

that lies on her surface by striking away the surface.

Then all shall perish.

The innocent, the sinful

but most of all,

the watchers!

I am condemned!

Scorned by the omnipotent Almighty;

cursed by all humanity;

denounced by my own account.

Never again will I be treated like a human being

for the sin I've just committed is unforgivable.

Until I die angels shall spit upon my person

in a frenzied reaction of disdain.

Respect has been stripped away from my life.

A Peeping Tom is virtuous compared to me.

A prostitute is pious compared to me.

A pervert is saintly compared to me.

A sadist is holy compared to me.

I am nothing more than a shameless libertine

doomed to crawl in the smut of the gutter.

Vulgar is my first and given name,

lewd is my baptized Christian name

and my true character is summed up

in my surname of horny.

I can be a dignitary in any whorehouse,

king of the porno films

or a VIP in a union of hustlers.

A pimp is above my station in the universe;

the only person more polluted than me

is a foul and filthy rapist.

Why did this have to happen?

Disgraced by a moment of weakness;

ill-famed in less than a second;

mortified before I could blink an eye.

Dear God, my Lord, hear my words.

Please punish me.

I ask you to please punish me.

Not by sending me to Hell

but by canceling my perpetual libido

and desexualizing me for all eternity.

Please have no pity for me

because I've forfeited all rights to orgasms.

To further my merited punishment

I shall ostracize myself

from the righteous world of Mankind;

blackball myself from ethical society;

excommunicate myself from moral life

for I've lost all sense of propriety!

Why do you turn away from me

and ignore the signals of suicide?

Why do you create the illusion of happiness

and foolishly convince yourself

that nothing is wrong?

Why do you believe that things will get better

while you do nothing to heal my wounds?

Why do you insist that life is wonderful

when a tragedy is being performed

before your very eyes?

Why do you have nightmares about my death

then tell yourself

that I am only going through a phase?

Must I die before you hear my cries?

Must a eulogy be given

before you acknowledge my solitude?

Must I be buried before you see my frustration?

Must my tombstone give evidence of my despair?

Must I be a memory

before you think of ways to help?

Look at me

and see the hunger for love upon my face.

Look at me

and see the prison bars of loneliness in my eyes.

Look at me

and see ninety years of apathy

engraved on my frown.

Look at me

and see my youthfulness fade into oblivion.

Look at me

and see your follower

fall from life's tightrope willfully.

Why must you wait until it's too late?

Why must it come as a shock?

Why must you say "If only I had known"?

Why must you face reality

when my ordeal is finally over?

Why must you try to understand

after my soul has perished to Hell?

You'll cry for the hungry children of Africa.

You'll pity the sick mothers of South America.

You'll worry about the homeless fathers of Asia.

You'll donate to charities

on the far side of the moon.

You'll save all the goddamn whales

in the Andromeda galaxy

but for me there's nothing.

Admitting my depression

questions your credibility as a Church.

Look at me!

Look at me!

For the love of God will you please look at me!

Let me know that you care.

The world took on

a disheartening perspective this morning.

I seem to be aware of the danger around me.

I am looking with apprehensive eyes

and not those of a carefree and lackadaisical nature.

I no longer see wonder in every little thing.

The drudgery and loathsomeness of living

has somehow awakened my sense of caution.

The environment of the streets is harsh and deadly.

I desire the safe isolation of my loving home.

Things around me seem threatening;

the Forest Of No Return would be safer to roam.

Life is not secure on the streets.

I am distressed because I am not on home ground

where I can call "safe" against the forces of ill-will.

I am walking in an uncharted

and unexplored territory

where the thought of the unknown

is far more sinister than the unknown itself.

I am afraid that I won't make it back home.

I might one day

disappear from the face of the earth without a trace
and no one would notice what happened to me.

Why should they?

On the streets

I am no longer a member of the family

where everyone worries about my welfare.

I am just one in a million frightened people

walking the impersonal streets of the city,

waiting for the worst to happen.

No one knows my name

or seems to care about me one way or another.

I am vulnerable for any kidnapper or assassin.

I hate walking the streets because nothing is mine.

Everything is unfamiliar and distant;

I can't leave my mark anywhere.

On the streets I don't exist;

I am a figment of my own imagination.

The streets overwhelm my fragile presence.

The steps I take never touch the pavement.

The movement of my body

cannot be seen with a telescope.

The memory of my achievements

is forgotten by the Earth.

The sound of my heart

becomes the pounding of the funeral drums.

The words I speak

are drowned out by the noise of violence.

My smile is shot down by the guns of despair.

My laugher is mistaken for hysterical cries.

The warmth of my touch

becomes frozen by the hostility in the air.

No one sees the compassion in my eyes,

the dignity in my countenance

or the superiority in my total manner.

On the streets

I learn that the world does not revolve around me.

I am not the center of the universe.

I am not the cutest, smartest or strongest.

I am not a superstar.

I am an ordinary person

who cannot shake the earth of my own garden.

I cannot succumb to the dastardly word "failure."
The idea of surrendering my lofty aspirations
to the imperial nation of broken dreams
must be scourged from my mind
and transformed into inspired hope.
The battle with frustration is a life long struggle
which bombards the moral fiber
with suspicious wounds.
Never will I conquer
the menacing warriors of pessimism
or the ominous knights of self-doubt
but I'll cross swords with these damnable foes
until their challenge of defeating my will
is eventually ended by the laughing Grim Reaper.
"Endure"
is the motto of my flesh embodied country
and the only word within my soul's constitution is
"Persevere"!
I will not let my dreams be trampled
by the hooves of futility.
Skepticism crushes the iron backbone

of inner strength;

disbelief stains faith's diaphanous frock;

uncertainty overflows the gourd of confidence

but with the intrepid feather of human pluck,

I can tickle any suicidal discouragement

to a jauntily blithesome death.

My heart is pulsating moxie fire,

illuminating the darkest crevices of human will.

I radiate with desire

to actualize transcendental dreams;

to skate on the Milky Way;

to prick a finger on Alpha Centauri;

to seek out Halley's Comet

and blow it out on half a breath.

I would travel to the outer gates of Hades

just to bark three times at Cerberus.

I believe that I can move continents with my hands

or change water into gold

because I have that gutsy determination to succeed.

Nothing in this rhapsody stifling world

can hinder me from accomplishing my sacred goal!

To order another copy of this book, send $15.00
plus $3.00 for shipping & handling to:

L I A PUBLISHING CO.
P.O. BOX 5373
NEW YORK, NY 10185-5373

New York State residents please add sales tax.
Checks or money orders only.

Please allow 3-4 weeks for delivery.

****
Organizations wishing to schedule a poetry
reading by Bernard Holland, please contact
L I A Publishing Co. by mail.